TENNIS GRAND SLAM

GLOBAL CITIZENS: SPORTS

CHERRY
LAKE
Publishing

Published in the United States of America by Cherry Lake Publishing
Ann Arbor, Michigan
www.cherrylakepublishing.com

Content Adviser: Liv Williams, Editor, www.iLivExtreme.com
Reading Adviser: Marla Conn, MS, Ed., Literacy specialist, Read-Ability, Inc.

Photo Credits: ©Victor Fraile/Alamy Stock Photo, cover; ©Zhukovsky/Dreamstime, 1, 9; ©Bain News
Service/Library of Congress/Reproduction No. LC-DIG-ggbain-09654, 5; ©Harris & Ewing/Library of
Congress/Reproduction No. LC-DIG-hec-31303, 6; ©Laborant/Shutterstock, 7; ©Leonard Zhukovsky/
Shutterstock, 8, 13, 15, 21; ©Jerry Coli/Dreamstime, 10; ©ZUMAPRESS.com/Keystone Pictures
USA/age footstock, 16; ©lev radin/Shutterstock, 19, 27, 28; ©Alison Young/Shutterstock, 20;
©Lucy Clark/Shutterstock, 22; ©Denis Stankovic/Shutterstock, 23; ©Rena Schild/Shutterstock, 24

Copyright ©2020 by Cherry Lake Publishing
All rights reserved. No part of this book may be reproduced or utilized in any form or by any means
without written permission from the publisher.

Library of Congress Cataloging-in-Publication Data

Names: Hellebuyck, Adam, author. | Deimel, Laura, author.
Title: Tennis grand slam / written by Adam Hellebuyck and Laura Deimel.
Description: Ann Arbor, Michigan : Cherry Lake Publishing, [2019] | Series: Global Citizens: Sports |
    Audience: Grades 4 to 6 | Includes bibliographical references and index.
Identifiers: LCCN 2019004216 | ISBN 9781534147508 (hardcover) | ISBN 9781534150362 (paperback) |
    ISBN 9781534148932 (pdf) | ISBN 9781534151796 (hosted ebook)
Subjects: LCSH: Tennis—Tournaments—Juvenile literature. | Social sciences—Juvenile literature.
Classification: LCC GV999 .H445 2019 | DDC 796.342—dc23
LC record available at https://lccn.loc.gov/2019004216

Cherry Lake Publishing would like to acknowledge the work of the Partnership for 21st Century Learning.
Please visit *www.p21.org* for more information.

Printed in the United States of America
Corporate Graphics

ABOUT THE AUTHORS

Laura Deimel is a fourth grade teacher and Adam Hellebuyck is a high school social studies
teacher at University Liggett School in Grosse Pointe Woods, Michigan. They have worked
together for the past 8 years and are thrilled they could combine two of their passions, reading
and sports, into this work.

TABLE OF CONTENTS

CHAPTER 1

History: From Hands to the Grand Slam

Tennis has a long and interesting history. It is played by millions and watched by millions of **spectators**. While there are hundreds of tournaments during the year, four major ones make up tennis's "Grand Slam": the Australian Open, the French Open, Wimbledon, and the U.S. Open.

The Beginning of Tennis

A form of tennis has been played since as early as the 11th and 12th centuries. The game began in France as *jeu de paume*, or "palm game." It quickly spread all over the world. Players hit

During the 1800s to mid-1900s, women played tennis in heavy full-length dresses!

the ball with their hands and not a racket. The game was usually played indoors by the royal family and nobles of the country. Over time, the game became more popular, and common people started to play it. As more people played, the game evolved. In the 1500s, people started returning the ball with rackets instead of their hands. The game has only changed a little since then.

The term *Grand Slam* was already being used in golf for any player who won the four major golf tournaments.

Starting the Grand Slam

There is no global tournament to determine the world's best tennis player. Instead, the International Lawn Tennis Federation, now called the International Tennis Federation (ITF), decided in the early 1920s to use four tournaments around the world to see who the best players were. The federation selected one tournament in Asia and the Pacific Ocean region: the Australian Open. It selected one tournament in the Americas: the U.S. Open. And it selected two tournaments in Europe: Wimbledon and the

Depending on the type of court being used, tennis balls before 1972 were either white or black.

The French Open is called the Tournoi de Roland-Garros in France. It is named after a famous French pilot who flew during World War I.

Wheelchair tennis was added to the Australian Open in 2002. It was added to the remaining three Grand Slam events by 2017.

French Open. Collectively, these four tournaments were called the Grand Slam. There is a Grand Slam for **singles**, **doubles**, juniors under the age of 18, and both men's and women's wheelchair players.

Types of Winners

A player who wins one or more Grand Slam tournaments can earn different titles. A player who wins one of the four tournaments is called a Grand Slam tournament winner. A player who wins each of the four tournaments during their tennis career earns

Steffi Graf of Germany earned a Calendar Golden Slam in 1988.

a Career Grand Slam. A player who wins each of the four tournaments in the same year earns the Grand Slam. Only six players have earned the Grand Slam in the same year in singles tennis. A player who wins all four Grand Slam tournaments plus the gold medal in tennis at the Olympic Games during the same year earns a Calendar Golden Slam. This is very rare. Steffi Graf of Germany is the only player to date to have done this.

Developing Questions

There are over 15,000 tennis tournaments around the world each year. Think about why four tournaments (the Australian Open, the French Open, Wimbledon, and the U.S. Open) were chosen to be the Grand Slam of tennis. Why were they chosen over the other tournaments? If you were in charge of today's ITF, would you keep these four tournaments? Would you select other tournaments? Why? Using your local library and the internet, find out more about tennis tournaments around the world. How are they different from the four Grand Slam tournaments?

CHAPTER 2

Geography: Around the World

Tennis is a popular sport all around the world. The Grand Slam tournaments are held in four countries on three continents.

Australia

The Australian Open is held in Melbourne, a city in southeastern Australia. The tournament is held in January. Since Australia is in the **Southern Hemisphere**, this means the tournament takes place in the summer.

Rafael Nadal and Roger Federer, two **all-star** tennis players, asked the organizers of the Australian Open to move the tournament date. They wanted it held in February so it was

MELBOURNE

The seasons in Australia and all the countries in the Southern Hemisphere are opposite those of the countries in the Northern Hemisphere.

farther away from the December holidays. This would give the players more time to celebrate holidays like Hanukkah and Christmas before taking part in the tournament. The organizers would not move the date. The reason? The Australian Open occurs during the country's summer vacation. If it were moved to February, many Australians would not be able to attend because they had to go to work or school.

France

The French Open is held in Paris, the capital of France. The tournament starts at the end of May and is held over a span of 2 weeks at the Roland-Garros stadium. The stadium is the smallest of the Grand Slam **venues**. Roland-Garros has 20 tennis courts, with three large stadiums that can only hold a few thousand spectators. The three stadiums used to not have roofs, so matches had to stop when it rained.

Since Roland-Garros is the smallest venue, tennis officials have wanted to move the French Open to a larger space. A larger space could hold more fans and let more matches happen at the same time. Many people want to keep the tournament at Roland-Garros because of its history and location in the center of Paris. Instead of moving the tournament, the organizers decided to expand the stadium and put in **retractable** roofs over the main courts. This means that future matches could be played in the rain!

The French Open used to be played on grass courts! It now uses clay courts.

Billie Jean King won the women's U.S. Open four times and helped make tennis popular for women in the United States.

United Kingdom

Wimbledon is held in London, the capital of the United Kingdom. It occurs during the first 2 weeks in July. Wimbledon is famous for its traditions. One tradition is that players must wear all white at the tournament. If a player does not, a referee can make him or her change before the match. Another tradition is for fans to eat strawberries and cream as a snack. Fans eat nearly 2 million strawberries and 2,000 gallons (7,571 liters) of cream at the tournament every year!

United States

The U.S. Open is held in New York City and begins on the last Monday of August. But it hasn't always been held there. The tournament has moved several times since it began in 1881. Newport, Rhode Island, was the first place it was held. In 1915, it moved to the West Side Tennis Club in Queens—one of the five **boroughs** in New York City—since many players and fans were in that area. Then, in 1978, the tournament moved just 3 miles (5 kilometers) away to the larger USTA Billie Jean King National Tennis Center.

Gathering and Evaluating Sources

Tennis fans from around the world travel to experience the Grand Slam matches in person. Each tournament has thousands of spectators. Study the data in the table below showing the number of people who attended each tournament. Which tournament had the highest attendance? Using your local library and the internet, try to figure out why that tournament had the most people.

2015 Grand Slam Attendance

Australian Open	*703,899*
French Open	*463,328*
Wimbledon	*484,391*
U.S. Open	*691,280*

CHAPTER 3

Civics: Scoring and Manners

Rules are very important in the game of tennis, particularly during the Grand Slam tournaments. There are many **regulations** for each tournament, addressing how each match is scored, the types of court surface the game is played on, and the **etiquette** players and fans must use in the game.

What's the Score?

Tennis matches are made up of games and sets. In order to win a match against another player, a male player must win three sets and a female player must win two. A set is made up of games. A player must win six games in order to win a set. A player has to win a set by two games to keep things fair.

The U.S. Open is the first of the four events in the Grand Slam to adopt the 25-second shot clock rule. This rule gives players only 25 seconds to serve the ball.

Players could be fined up to $20,000 for not being ready to play within 7 minutes of walking on court!

Each game is made up of four points. Zero points is called love. The first point is called 15, the second point is called 30, and the

A Romantic Game

Why is zero called "love" in tennis? Why is the scoring system so different from any other sport? Nobody really knows. One popular theory is that French people called no score an egg, because "0" looked like an egg. "Egg" in French is l'oeuf, which is pronounced similarly to the English word love. As for the scoring system, many believe it might be related to using clock faces as a way to keep score.

Serena Williams broke a few rules during the 2018 U.S. Open, which resulted in her losing the match. Do you think this was fair?

Wimbledon is the only tournament in the Grand Slam that has a strict all-white clothing rule. This even includes the soles of their sneakers!

Tennis players could be fined for a number of things, including, using foul language, yelling, and smashing their racket on the court.

third point is called 40. The fourth point wins the game, although a player needs to win by two points.

Courtside Manners

Tennis players in the Grand Slam tournaments must follow a code of etiquette when they play. For example, players must not make loud noises, they must dress professionally, they must show up on time, and they must be honest and fair during each match. Players are not allowed to distract their opponent in any way

The average age of tennis fans who attended the 2017 U.S. Open was 42 years old. Only 4 percent of fans were under the age of 18.

during a match and must shake their opponent's hand at the end of the match. There are even rules that specify where players must hang their towels at the end of each match!

Spectators also have to follow rules of etiquette. They must stay quiet during each game and can only cheer after a point is scored. Fans must stay in their seats until two sets have been played. Their phones need to be set to silent during each match. Fans are allowed to take pictures during each match, but they cannot use a flash since it could distract the players. Wimbledon has the most serious rules for spectators.

Developing Claims and Using Evidence

Pete Sampras is a famous American tennis player who won a record 14 Grand Slam tournaments during his career. However, he never won the French Open. Using your local library and the internet, learn more about Pete Sampras and how he played tennis. Also, learn more about how tennis is played at the French Open. Why do you think Pete Sampras never won the event?

CHAPTER 4

Economics: Paid to Play

While many athletes play because they love the game, they are also paid for their work. This is because they are professional athletes. They earn this money in different ways.

Prize Money

When athletes compete in Grand Slam tournaments, they have a chance to win **prize money**. Winning any round of a Grand Slam tournament can earn an athlete money. For example, in the 2018 U.S. Open, a player who lost in the first round earned $54,000. A player who lost in the second round earned $93,000, while the **semifinals** loser earned $925,000. The tournament winner earned $3,800,000. Also in 2018, the winner of the Australian Open earned $1,901,113 (in U.S. dollars). The winner

Players who lose their first round during the U.S. Open still take home a lot of money.

of the French Open earned $2,489,955, and the winner of Wimbledon received $2,869,861.

Paying the Players

In order to pay all the athletes who participate in the Grand Slam series, each tournament needs to gather a large **purse**. All of the tournaments collect sponsors. Sponsors pay to advertise their goods at the event. The tournament organizers call these sponsors "partners." For example, Citizen Watch used to be the

ESPN, a popular sports channel, paid $825 million to have exclusive rights to televise the U.S. Open.

official timer of tennis matches at the U.S. Open. In 2018, Rolex offered more money to the U.S. Open organization to become the official timer. Now Rolex is the official timekeeper of the U.S. Open, the Australian Open, and Wimbledon.

Taking Informed Action

Would you like to play tennis? Did you know that each of the four Grand Slam tournaments also hosts a tournament for players under the age of 18? You can learn more about how to get involved through the International Tennis Federation Juniors website!

Sponsor partners come from all over the world and offer all kinds of different goods. These goods do not have to be related to tennis. Companies might sell ice cream, bottled water, and pasta. Banks and credit card companies in the host countries partner with the tournaments to help pay the purse, as do automakers and airlines.

Clothing companies also partner with the tournaments, offering more than just money for the purse. For example, Ralph Lauren partnered with Wimbledon to provide the clothing for all the officials and staff of the tournament. While they still wear the traditional dark green and purple tie, Ralph Lauren changed the rest of the uniform to navy blue jackets and cream-colored pants. These officials are walking advertisements for Ralph Lauren during Wimbledon.

Communicating Conclusions

Unlike many other sports, the prize money for Grand Slam tournaments is the same for men and women athletes. The U.S. Open was the first of the tournaments to give equal prize money to men and women. It began this in 1973. Why do you think the prize money in other sporting tournaments is different for men and women? Is this fair? Why or why not? Share your thoughts with a friend or family member. Ask them what they think.

Think About It

The Hawk-Eye is a computer and video system that helps decide whether balls are in or out of bounds in Grand Slam tournaments. Players like this system because it lets them challenge officials' calls they disagree with. However, some experts wonder how accurate the system really is because no data on it has been shared. How could you test how accurate the Hawk-Eye really is? How would you create your own data on the Hawk-Eye?

For More Information

Further Reading

Hubbard, Crystal. *The Story of Tennis Champion Arthur Ashe.* New York, NY: Lee & Low Books, 2018.

Porterfield, Jason. *Maria Sharapova: Tennis Grand Slam Champion.* New York, NY: Rosen Education Service, 2019.

Websites

Kiddle—Grand Slam (Tennis) Facts for Kids
https://kids.kiddle.co/Grand_Slam_(tennis)
This site gives more information on each of the four Grand Slam tournaments.

United States Tennis Association—Getting Started
https://www.usta.com/en/home/play/lots-of-ways-to-play/youth.html
This site shows how people of any age can play tennis for fun or in competitions.

GLOSSARY

all-star (AWL-stahr) outstanding

boroughs (BUR-ohz) the five main sections of New York City

doubles (DUHB-uhlz) a tennis match played between two pairs of players

etiquette (ET-ih-kit) polite ways people act

prize money (PRIZE MUHN-ee) money given to the winner of a game, match, or event

purse (PURS) the total amount of money given out as prizes in a competition

regulations (reg-yuh-LAY-shuhnz) rules

retractable (rih-TRAKT-uh-buhl) something that can be extended or pulled back

semifinals (SEM-ee-fye-nuhlz) games or matches in a tournament right before the finals or championship

singles (SING-guhlz) a tennis match played between two players

Southern Hemisphere (SUHTH-urn HEM-ih-sfeer) the half of the Earth south of the equator

spectators (SPEK-tay-turz) people who watch an event

venues (VEN-yooz) locations where events are held

INDEX